Twelve Truths About Sex for Tweens and Teens

Preparation for Making an Abstinence Promise

Roger Sonnenberg

WESTBOW
PRESS®
A DIVISION OF THOMAS NELSON
& ZONDERVAN

WestBow Press books may be ordered through booksellers or by contacting:

WestBow Press
A Division of Thomas Nelson & Zondervan
1663 Liberty Drive
Bloomington, IN 47403
www.westbowpress.com
1 (866) 928-1240

ISBN: 978-1-5127-8861-7 (sc)
ISBN: 978-1-5127-8860-0 (e)

Library of Congress Control Number: 2017910981

Print information available on the last page.

WestBow Press rev. date: 07/19/2017

About the Author

Roger Sonnenberg was a pastor to a large parish in California. He holds a master of divinity degree from Concordia Seminary in St. Louis, Missouri, as well as a master's degree in psychotherapy from the American Institute of Family Relations in Los Angeles, California. He served as a part-time professor in the graduate marriage and family program at Concordia University at Seward, Nebraska, and an adjunct professor at Concordia University, Irvine, California. He lectures and conducts seminars throughout the United States and Canada on sexuality, marriage, and family relations.

He served as the first vice president of the Pacific Southwest District (PSD) of the Lutheran Church, Missouri Synod, as well as chairman of the board of directors of the PSD. He served as chairman of Family Shield in St. Louis, Missouri, and as a member of the Nightlight Adoption board of Orange County, California. He has authored many articles, studies, and books, including *Parenting with Purpose* and *Parenting with Values*, (two video-based parenting programs), *501 Ways to Love Your Wife and Children, 501 Ways to Love Your Grandkids* and *Their Parents, Human Sexuality, A Christian Perspective* (Concordia Publishing House, St. Louis, MO), and *Advent and Lenten Worship Services* (2008, 2009 Creative Communications, St. Louis, MO). He writes regularly for magazines and publications throughout the United States.

Roger and his wife, Robin, have been married for thirty-eight years and have one son, Jacob, who works as an analyst for a hedge fund in Manhattan, New York.

Cartoonist: Kara Dannenbring is a prize-winning cartoonist who contributes frequently to newspapers in Orange County, California, and throughout the United States.

Layout and Designer: Karen Hein McBride teaches desktop publishing at a local university and is a published author of technology-focused resources for educators.

This Book is for parents, grandparents, teachers, and others who want to help guide their children, grandchildren, or students into a God-pleasing understanding of sex and sexuality. There are twelve truths, followed by some facts, suggestions, and a biblical study. At the end of the book there are suggestions for parents and their tweens/teens, as well as for the church and its young people on how to conduct an abstinence pledge ceremony.

Definitions:

- **Truths** = known facts substantiated by evidence
- **Tweens** = a child between middle childhood and adolescence, usually between eight and twelve years (although this course is not recommended for anyone under eleven)
- **Teens** = those from thirteen to nineteen who think they know everything they need to know about sex

Why the Book?

David Walsh, media expert, said, "He who tells the story, dictates the culture" *(David Walsh, Presentation at LCMS Pastor's Conference, Palm Springs, 2009)*. We have no one to blame but ourselves if we do not tell the truths we know about sex and sexuality to our tweens and teenagers. When we do not share the *real truth*, we farm it out to others (i.e., the media) to teach them, and unfortunately, their lessons are not only often incorrect but extremely harmful.

This book attempts to help anyone who has an impact on any tween or teenager to openly discuss and study twelve important truths about sex and sexuality. It is my prayer and goal that as you discuss these truths, you will help dictate the culture—one that is healthier and more attuned to God's principles.

The twelve truths are short in duration because studies tell us that today's young people have difficulty spending long periods of time concentrating on any given subject. After all, they belong to a new generation of high technology, where everything is immediate and fast moving. Our goal is to engage in discussion on one important truth daily or each week, (however you choose to set up your lessons). The truth is always accompanied with some additional facts. You are asked to quickly read through those facts, considering the questions at the beginning of each lesson.

You and your tween/teenager are encouraged to take the following actions with each lesson. Once you've completed the lesson, sign your names at the bottom of the lesson and the date on which you completed it

1. Read aloud the truth.
2. Read together the truths that follow (some discussion may take place, especially those truths that are in the form of a question).
3. Consider all or as many as you wish of the discussion questions.
4. Discuss all or as many as you wish of the Bible questions.

As you look at the cartoon introducing each lesson, introduce the lesson by role playing or answering the questions given on each cartoon page.

There are also resources listed at the end of each lesson for those using this program in the school (or home). Many of the suggestions are special programs available from those specializing in abstinence teaching (i.e., Pam Stenzel), as well as video clips from such sources as: Faith Visuals, YouTube, GodTube (tangle), SermonSpice, special news programs, and the Internet. The author of this book has accumulated many additional suggested resources that can be used for each section. If you want this list, you may contact the author (sonnenr@aol.com). It is highly recommended you use some of these resources to connect with the students in more ways than via a written lesson. Remember, tweens/teens today are highly technical *and* are very familiar with many of the sources listed (i.e., YouTube).

As you review some of the thoughts featured at the beginning of each lesson, they may seem unbelievable and even scary; however, all the stats are substantiated through reliable surveys and studies. Many of these facts are changing even as you're considering them, which makes the information more alarming and signals a still greater need for these discussions to take place. So get started, and as serious and alarming as some of these thoughts may be, remember, our sexuality is not shameful or dirty; it's beautiful and God-given!

Warning! Some of the terminology and descriptive words may seem startling and out of place in a religious setting. However, in order to be relevant to many of today's tweens/teens, it is necessary to use the terminology and language they are being exposed to on a regular basis. Be assured, the author in no way wants to offend any of the participants.

Twelve Studies

Chapter 1

The Fool Says in His Heart, "There Is No God"

Truth: The gifts of sex and sexuality point to divine design.

Consider the following statements and questions that speak to this truth.

1. Do you agree or disagree with the statement?
2. Does the statement prompt any special feelings within you (e.g., fear, laughter, disbelief)?
3. What additional questions come to mind after reading the statement?

Have You Heard?

- Sex is not dirty. It's one of God's greatest gifts. What makes it one of God's greatest gifts?
- Everything about the human body, including being sexual and having the ability to reproduce, proves divine design. What other parts of the human body prove divine design?
- Though sex is a gift and can produce much pleasure in marriage, it is never to be glorified to be godlike in its own right. Besides a husband and wife enjoying sexual pleasure, what are other God-given reasons for marriage?

Proof to Consider

Want some proof for the existence of God? Follow your father's sperm as it travels to your mother's egg and finally implants itself, along with the egg, into the uterus.

- Being sexual, Dad and Mom are attracted to each other.
- With excitement, the creation of an erection takes place.
- Millions of sperm, stored in the epididymis, are released into the vas deferens.
- The vas deferens keeps the sperm speeding forward as it secretes a fluid that makes it more motile.
- At the end of the vas deferens are glands called seminal vesicles that produce additional seminal fluid for motility.
- The sperm enters the prostate gland, where it is joined by milky white fluid.
- Before this happens, however, the Cowper's glands have prepared the road by producing a lubricant known as preejaculation. This fluid coats the lining of the urethra and neutralizes acids in the urethra, making it a safer environment for the sperm.
- Through the miracle of ejaculation, the erect penis places the semen into the vagina.
- It passes through the cervix and the uterus, maybe even winking at the uterus and saying, "I'll be back later, if it all goes well."
- The semen races to find a partner to hook up with—an egg.
- Upon finding the egg, a single sperm attaches itself, coating the egg with a special fluid that keeps other suitors out.
- Shortly afterward, the fertilized egg journeys downward into the uterus, where the woman's body has prepared, through menstruation, a comfortable and safe home for implantation and growth for the next nine months.

It is all very good, just as the word says, "God saw all that He had made, and it was very good" (Genesis 1:31). Purposeful design. No accident. Impossible through some evolutionary process!

Some Discussion

1. An "accident" is a happening that is not expected, foreseen, or intended. As you review the simple facts of the sperm's journey to the egg, can you explain how such a journey could occur by accident, without planning and design from a divine Creator?
2. The Cowper's glands produce a lubricant known as preejaculation fluid that coats the lining of the uterus and neutralizes acids in the urethra. This makes it a safe environment for the sperm and lubricates the penis and vagina during intercourse. What kind of fool would say the Cowper's glands came about by an evolutionary process? How correct was the psalmist when he said, "I praise You because I am fearfully and wonderfully made" (Psalm 139:14)?
3. Chromosomes from both the sperm and the egg come together upon conception. This combination creates an individual person who shares features of both parents. What features do you have from your father? Your mother?

Some of God's Word

1. True or false? Adam and Eve were sexual and had sex before the fall of humankind. Read Genesis 1:27–28.
2. Read Psalm 14:1. What kind of faith would be required to believe that all the intricacies of reproduction could take place without a divine Creator?
3. Read Psalm 139:13–15. Name a few of the facts of reproduction you feel clearly indicate a divine Creator. When God saw everything He had made, He saw it was good (Genesis 1:28).
4. According to Genesis 1:27–28, how were male and female created? Define in your own words the "image of God." The truth is that when a husband and a wife come together physically, emotionally, and spiritually through sexual intercourse, they reflect the "image of God" in a way greater than when they are separate.
5. Study 1 Corinthians 6:19–20. How do we honor God sexually with our bodies?

Additional Video Clips for this Lesson (in Classroom or Home)

- ☑ human reproduction fertilization (YouTube)
- ☑ fertilization (YouTube)
- ☑ thoughts on sex (SermonSpice) (Note how confused people are today about the gift of sex.)
- ☑ What is sacred? (Faith Visuals) (Note how God makes a person sacred—not only his or her soul but his or her body as well.)

Role Play

What do you think the winning sperm is saying to the egg? And what about the losers? What are they saying?

Chapter 2

Stand Up and Shout, "I Won!"

Truth: Out of the millions of sperm racing for your mother's egg, you won.

Consider the following statements and questions that further speak to this truth.

1. Do you agree or disagree with the statement?
2. Does the statement prompt any special feelings within you (e.g., fear, laughter, disbelief)?
3. What additional questions come to mind after reading the statement?

What Do You Think?

1. Most men average per ejaculate
   a. several thousand sperm
   b. millions of sperm
   c. hundreds of sperm
   a. one per second since the previous ejaculation

2. After the sperm takes off from the epididymis, on average, how long does it take to get to the Fallopian tubes?
   a. 2 to 3 minutes
   b. 1 minute
   c. 15 minutes to 2 days
   b. 5 minutes to 68 minutes

(The answers are 1-b and 2-d)

- Scripture says, "For He chose us in Him before the creation of the world to be holy and blameless in His sight. In love He predestined us to be adopted as His sons through Jesus Christ, in accordance with His pleasure and will" (Ephesians 1:4–5). Do you think God knew about your conception before it happened?
- You are a winner twice over. God was not only intricately involved in the race of your father's sperm to your mother's egg, but He was also involved, even before your conception, in your salvation. Why do you think God cared for you so much?
- Put on the party hats! Bring out the balloons! Don't ever let anyone tell you you're not special. What should this do for your self-esteem?

Some Discussion

1. In some relationships, one of the persons may feel the other has value only if sexual favors are given. Knowing what you do about your conception as well as your salvation, what's wrong with such thinking?
2. Recent data is showing that many young people are having plastic surgery (e.g., to have larger breasts). Though some plastic surgery may be legitimate, what do you think this indicates about a person's self-esteem and God's design?
3. Answer: "My self esteem comes from …"?

Some of God's Word

1. Our winning the sperm race should make us stand up and shout, "I won!" but with humility. Read Psalm 139:16. Who ordained your days? Who always gets the praise?

2. Our salvation through Jesus Christ should also make us stand up and shout, "I'm a winner!" However, once again, who should be praised? Read Ephesians 2:8–10. How are we to praise Him not only for our conception but also for our salvation (v. 10)?

3. Read 1 Peter 2:9–10. But read it in the first-person point of view instead of the third ("I" instead of "you"). "I am a chosen person, a royal priesthood ..."

4. Read Jeremiah 29:11. What plans do you think God has for you regarding your future? Do you think He has plans for you to be a husband or wife or father or mother? In order that these plans might come to fruition, what kinds of things does God want you to do physically, emotionally, and spiritually?

Additional Video Clips for This Lesson (in Classroom or Home)

☑ Susan Boyle (YouTube): We often judge others by their outward appearances and miss what's most important—what's inside.

☑ body image statistics (GodTube/tangle)

Completed: _____   _____

         Student Signature & Date of Completion   Parent/Teacher Signature & Date of Completion

Role Play

In what ways does the cartoon correctly depict common ways in which many learn about sex and sexuality?

Chapter 3

"Love Handle" or "Love Map"?

Truth: Formed early in life, people have "love maps" that determine what they enjoy sexually and erotically.

Consider the following statements and questions that further speak to this truth.

1. Do you agree or disagree with the statement?
2. Does the statement prompt any special feelings within you (e.g., fear, laughter, disbelief)?
3. What additional questions come to mind after reading the statement?

What's in a Word?

- A favorite term, *love handle,* refers to excess weight around the waist or elsewhere that a lover can grab hold of. What do you think? Is it more difficult for a person to change his or her physical well-being than his or her thinking? Through exercise and diet, one can get rid of one's love handle. A person's "love map" is a bit more complicated and harder to change.
- A *love map* is the template formed in a person between the ages of five and eight, deciding whether a specific situation is arousing or not (coined by John Money). Do you recall any of the information you were taught about sex and sexuality at an early age?
- The love map is sometimes referred to as the "Rorschach love blot," which is a psychological test of personality in which a subject's interpretations of different abstract designs are analyzed. For fun, research what a Rorschach picture looks like.
- A love map can be distorted when
  - a family does not talk about sex or casts a negative judgment about anything sexual;
  - there are early sexual experiences that involve shame or fear;
  - there is early exposure to pornography, or
  - there is physical and sexual abuse.

When people have unresolved sexual issues, their love maps will entice them to search out answers or experiences that will satisfy their curiosity. What vehicles are now available to almost everyone to search out questions they might have regarding sex and sexuality?

Some Discussion

1. A person's love map is shaped by both positive and negative factors. Can you think of some positive and negative factors that have influenced your love map?
2. A love map is a template in the brain or the mind depicting the idealized lover. Describe what you believe is an idealized lover.
3. Sex education is a comprehensive program from cradle to grave. At this time in your life, what are some things you hope to learn about sex and your sexuality?

Some of God's Word

1. What are some biblical truths that are hopefully ingrained in every person's love map (Genesis 1:27b–28; Genesis 2:20a–24; 1 Corinthians 7:1–2; Hebrews 13:4)?
2. Read 1 Corinthians 13:4–8 for a description of an idealized lover.

3. Though a person's "love map" may have been skewed for a variety of reasons, what do we know can happen according to Philippians 4:13 and Romans 8:31–32?

Additional Resources for This Lesson (in Classroom or Home):

☑ Two books for parents and children—Concordia Publishing House: *How You Are Changing and Sex and the New You* (Boy's and Girl's Edition).

  ☑ *Man on the Street* (SermonSpice). Some of the people's love maps are mixed up.

Completed: _____   _____

  Student Signature & Date of Completion   Parent/Teacher Signature & Date of Completion

Role Play: How does the cartoon depict the confusion many have regarding how far to go in dating?

Chapter 4

Touching? Oral Sex? What Is Abstinence?

Truth: **Abstinence is abstaining from any kind of sexual relationship with another person.**

Consider the following statements and questions, which further speak to this truth:

1. Do you agree or disagree with the statement?
2. Does the statement prompt any special feelings within you (i.e., fear, laughter, unbelief)?
3. What additional questions come to mind after reading the statement?

Did You Know?

- Abstinence involves both outercourse and intercourse. Can you define the two words: outercourse and intercourse?
- A sexual relationship involves more than vaginal intercourse. It can also include outercourse: oral sex and mutual masturbation. Both oral sex and mutual masturbation have the same outcome—sexual activity that elicits a strong physical and emotional response. When most public schools speak of abstinence, do you think they include outercourse?
- Outercourse includes everything other than vaginal intercourse. It is an expression of love in ways other than through penile penetration, such as stroking and touching each other's bodies. In what ways are both intercourse and outercourse forms of having sex?

Studies tell us that large numbers of teenagers are involved in oral sex and mutual masturbation, and they believe two things:
1. Both acts are safe sex.
2. They are still practicing abstinence.

Though oral sex may prevent pregnancy, it doesn't prevent the spread of certain STIs (Sexually Transmitted Infections), For example, human papilloma virus (genital warts) is viral and can be spread by skin-to-skin contact. Oral sex is hardly free of skin contact! It should not surprise us that over 50 percent of all sexually active people have STI, HPV.

Some Discussion

1. In what ways has the definition of sex been challenged over the last twenty years? Define sex according to most people today.
2. Do you know that both herpes and HPV (human papilloma virus) can be spread without vaginal intercourse? There are two strains of herpes: type 1 (HSV-1), and type 2 (HSV-2). Both viruses can be transmitted in a variety of ways, including kissing, touching, etc. Since both of these STIs are viral, what does it mean as far as a cure? Why do you think most educators and parents don't talk about these dangers?
3. Many young people talk about being abstinent and yet engage in oral sex and mutual masturbation. In what way is the secular definition of abstinence different from what many Christians define as abstinence?
4. Give your personal definition of sex and of abstinence.

Some of God's Word

1. What is God's definition of sex according to Genesis 2:24? The term "one flesh" indicates that they were in union physically, emotionally, and spiritually.

2. Read Genesis 4:1, 17, 25. In your own words, describe what you think it means when God speaks of "knowing" a person. The Hebrew word used for "know" is "Yaw-dah." It means "to be known, be or become known, be revealed." Yada sex is fully sensuous, fully receiving, fully entering, fully knowing, and fully being known.

3. St. Paul spoke against sex outside marriage. What advice does he give in 1 Corinthians 7:2?

4. What words did Jesus speak to the woman who was having sex outside marriage (John 8:11)? What similar words does Jesus speak to any of us who have sinned sexually? How is one able to start anew and not continue repeating the same sin over and over (Romans 6:5-7)?

Additional Resources for This Lesson (in Classroom or Home):

☑ Pam Stenzel, DVD, *Sex, Love, and Relationships.* (This is a four-part series, making it perfect for an additional teaching aid in addressing the issues of the physical, emotional, and spiritual aspects of sexuality. Though you need to view all four parts of this series, divide it up according to how it best fits your topic of discussion each week. Stenzel has wonderful discussion questions as well as activities to help the participants understand important truths.)

☑ *It's Just Sex* (SermonSpice)

Completed: _____   _____
       Student Signature & Date of Completion   Parent/Teacher Signature & Date of Completion

Role Play: Have you seen a similar scene in your neighborhood? In what ways do you think the cartoon correctly depicts not only animals but also some people?

Chapter 5

People Not Animals

Truth: **People having sex act like animals when they act on instinct or feelings instead of love**

Consider the following statements and questions that further speak to this truth:

1. Do you agree or disagree with the statement?
2. Does the statement prompt any special feelings within you (i.e., fear, laughter, unbelief)?
3. What additional questions come to mind after reading the statement?

Have You Heard?

- Someone said, "People are acting like animals." Describe in what way.
- Some people do act like animals when it comes to their sexuality. Can you give some examples?
- Some people hook up via e-mail and meet in the local mall bathroom to breed. Do you know of anyone who has done this?
- They text each other or contact each other through Twitter, asking for sexual favors, without even an "I love you," "I care about you," or "thank you." How would you describe such "love"?
- A male dog doesn't know how to use e-mail, Twitter, or text messaging, but if it smells a female dog in heat, it will break down a fence in order to breed, without even an "I love you" or "I care for you." What makes animals different than human beings?
- Animal shelters are filled with unwanted dogs and cats because of it.
- In 2008, 50 percent of all children were born to single moms (Emily Badger, The Washington Post,, December 18, 2014, pg 17). Is this bad or good?
- A statement such as, "You can't expect young people today to remain abstinent until marriage" suggests young people are no better than animals, driven by instinct instead of a desire for relationship. Do you agree or disagree? Why?
- Sex is not a hormonal problem you can't control. You *do* have a choice. What did God put into human beings that gives man a choice?

Some Discussion

1. What message is being conveyed when high schools and other institutions pass out condoms to whoever wants them?
2. What's different about relationships among human beings than those between animals?
3. Describe behaviors human beings are doing today in the area of sex that resemble actions of animals.
4. In what ways has the world of technology changed sexual mores and habits in the twenty-first century?

Some of God's Word

1. How did God create humans to be different than animals (Genesis 1:26; 2:20b–23)?
2. What does St. Paul remind us happens when people disconnect themselves from God (Romans 1:20–21, 24)?
3. Though some may suggest it is illogical and impossible for young people to abstain from sexual activity before marriage, what does God's word remind us of (Matthew 19:26)?
4. Read 2 Corinthians 5:17. Why is it true that non-Christians may not be able to abstain from sex outside of marriage but Christians can be obedient to God's word?

Additional Resources for This Lesson (in Classroom or Home):

☑ Pam Stenzel, *Character Matters*. Use the portion that is most appropriate and fits into your time frame.

☑ *Thoughts on Sex* (SermonSpice)

Completed: _____   _____

                Student Signature & Date of Completion   Parent/Teacher Signature & Date of Completion

Role Play: What do you know about any of the STDs being hurled at those in the foxhole? Do you know of any that are not depicted in the cartoon?

Chapter 6

STDs, STIs...
Whatever You Want to Call Them

Truth: There are over thirty sexually transmitted infections, with consequences ranging from sterility to death.

Consider the following statements and questions that further speak to this truth:

1. Do you agree or disagree with the statement?
2. Does the statement prompt any special feelings within you (i.e., fear, laughter, unbelief)?
3. What additional questions come to mind after reading the statement?

Did You Know?

- Sexually transmitted diseases (STDS) are diseases that are spread through sexual intercourse and outercourse. What sexual activities might be considered as "outercourse" if it is defined as everything outside sexual intercourse?

- The term *STDs* has been renamed STIs. Why? Would you believe that the word *disease* sounded too frightening and so some suggested it would be better to use the word *infection*? Strange. One can define a disease as something that is harmful or destructive to the body. STIs are scary. They are harmful, causing many serious consequences, from sterility to death. What do you think? Is it better to call them STIs instead of STDs?

- Why do you think one out of three teenagers has contracted or will contract an STI?

- There are more than thirty sexually transmitted diseases. Some of the major ones include: chlamydia, human papilloma virus (genital warts), gonorrhea, HIV/AIDS, syphilis, trichomoniasis, chancroid, and cytomegalovirus. Some are viral (noncurable), and some are bacterial (treatable). Do you know which ones are treatable and which ones are not?

- One of the most common bacterial STDs is chlamydia. Though it is treatable with drugs, the more times one contracts the disease, the greater chance of permanent infertility. Do you think this might be the reason for so much infertility in the United States?

- Over 50 percent of all sexually active people have human papilloma virus (HPV). It is viral, so it is with you forever. It is the number-one cause of cervical cancer in women. It can be spread through skin-to-skin contact, meaning it can spread through intercourse and outercourse. Gardasil, a recent HPV vaccine, protects women from four of the seventy HPV strains (6, 11, 16, 18). It is also a vaccine which protects boys from cancer due to HPV infection. Would you recommend that parents protect their daughters and sons by having them vaccinated?

- Genital herpes, a viral STD, has two strains: type 1 (HSV-1), and type 2 (HSV-2). Both can be transmitted in a variety of ways, including kissing, touching, etc. Type 2 is especially dangerous for an unborn child of an infected mother.

- HIV/AIDS (acquired immune deficiency syndrome) is viral and transmitted from semen to blood or blood to blood contact. The development of powerful drugs has extended the lives of many infected AIDS patients; however, do they cure the infection?

- There is only one sure way of avoiding STD infection—abstinence.

Some Discussion

1. If, indeed, an average sexually active person of thirty has had over twenty-eight sexual relationships, and if over 50 percent of all sexually active people are infected with HPV, what are the chances of not being infected with this disease or some other STI?

2. With the introduction of the Gardasil vaccine for the major HPV strains causing cervical cancer and genital warts, would you recommend the vaccination for any teenage girl? Even though the young lady remains abstinent until marriage, what are the chances her future husband will have done the same? How about for boys?

3. A favorite sexual practice among many young people today is oral sex, thinking it is "safe sex." What's wrong with such thinking, and what STIs could one get from this sexual practice?

Some Bible Truths

1. Chlamydia is treatable with drugs; however, many live infected without knowing it. The consequence of repeated chlamydia infection is sterility. In what way does this go against God's original plan for His people (Genesis 1:28)?
2. Compare Matthew 21:12–13 with 1 Corinthians 6:19–20. In what way was the defilement of God's temple similar to what St. Paul warns of in 1 Corinthians 6:19–20?
3. Read Galatians 6:7–8. Some would say that HIV/AIDS is a consequence of sinful behavior, especially among homosexuals. Agree or disagree? Why does any kind of illness or disease exist in our world? A similar question was asked in John 9:1–5. How did Jesus answer the question?
4. What promise is given to us in Revelation 21:4 regarding HIV/AIDS or any disease?

Additional Resources for This Lesson (in Classroom or Home):

☑ Pam Stenzel, *Sex, Love, and Relationships* (Part 1, Physical Consequences).
☑ Pam Stenzel, *Love Lessons, Purity is Possible Curriculum—Faith*.

Completed: _____   _____
               Student Signature & Date of Completion   Parent/Teacher Signature & Date of Completion

Role Play: Who seems most surprised in the picture? Why?

Chapter 7

Using a "Jimmy Hat" for "Safe Sex"

Truth: **Safe sex is not a condom.**

Consider the following statements and questions that further speak to this truth:

1. Do you agree or disagree with the statement?
2. Does the statement prompt any special feelings within you (i.e., fear, laughter, unbelief)?
3. What additional questions come to mind after reading the statement?

What Do You Think?

- What's the first thing that comes to mind when you hear "safe sex"? Condoms! Why?
- Condoms are also known as rubbers, rain coats, love gloves, Jimmy hats, Pardas, and French letters. Can you think of any other names?
- A condom fits over the penis, blocking the sperm from being released into the vagina. If so, why does pregnancy sometimes occur?
- Condoms are made of several substances, from latex to polyurethane.
- "Use a Jimmy hat for safe sex!" "Lawyers, get ready to sue someone. Jimmy hats do not always offer safe sex'!" As a lawyer, who would you sue first, the condom manufacturer or the consumer?
- The average failure rate for male condom usage is 12 to 20 percent, depending on the study (meaning for every 100 women whose partners use condoms, twelve to twenty of them will become pregnant during a year of typical use). Do these statistics surprise you? Why or why not?
- Condom usage is as old as the hills. Ancient Egyptians used linen sheaths, and the most famous lover of all, Casanova, used animal intestines to prevent pregnancy and disease.
- Besides male condoms, there are female condoms—a loose-fitting pouch that fits into the vagina. Why do you think a female condom might be less effective in preventing pregnancy?

Some Discussion

1. The two primary reasons people use condoms is to prevent pregnancy and reduce the spread of STIs. If a condom provides "safe sex," why might pregnancy still occur 12 to 20 percent of the time? Condoms do not prevent the spread of HPV (genital warts) or genital herpes. What kind of disclaimer do you think condom advertisers should give regarding their product?
2. Considering that the diameter of the HIV virus is 450 times smaller than the head of a human sperm and that condoms are known to have "voids" (holes), why might the use of condoms be like playing Russian roulette when it comes to preventing HIV/AIDS?
3. Complete the following statement: "Son (daughter), safe sex is …"

Some of God's Word

1. Dr. David Walsh says, "He who tells the story, dictates the culture." What's wrong with the story being told by schools and health clinics as they pass out free condoms? Read Hosea 4:6. Describe the ignorance being passed along in today's message of condom usage.
2. When and for what reasons might condom usage be appropriate in a marriage relationship (Ephesians 5:25)?
3. What's wrong with the following statement: "If you love me, you'll have sex with me, and besides, you don't have to worry; I have a condom" (1 Corinthians 13:6)?

4. Confessing Jesus as Savior sets us free from sin, death, and the power of the devil (John 8:32). His truth gives us eternal life and life "to the full" (John 10:10). How does God's truth about sex and the use of this gift give life "to the full"?

Additional Resources for This Lesson (in Classroom or Home):

☑ Pam Stenzel, *Sex, Love and Relationships*, (Part 1, Physical Consequences).

☑ *Man on the Street* (SermonSpice)

Completed: _____   _____

　　　　　　　Student Signature & Date of Completion　　　　　Parent/Teacher Signature & Date of Completion

Role Play: In what way does the man in the cartoon adequately reflect what many young people go through when it comes to masturbation?

Chapter 8

Autoeroticism or Masturbation

Truth: **Masturbation is the stimulation of one's sexual organs, usually to orgasm, and is a common sexual practice among men and women.**

Consider the following statements and questions that further speak to this truth.

1. Do you agree or disagree with the statement?
2. Does the statement prompt any special feelings within you (i.e., fear, laughter, unbelief)?
3. What additional questions come to mind after reading the statement?

Did You Know?

- No! Autoeroticism is not having sex while in an automobile. Then what is it?
- Masturbation (a.k.a., autoeroticism)
- Why do you think masturbation is the sexual behavior people are most secretive and ashamed about?
- The facts are that 97 percent of all males masturbate and 83 percent of all females. Do you believe these statistics? If so, why not?
- Masturbation does not cause insanity, nor does it cause you to grow hair on your palms. Do you think it harms anyone?

Some Discussion

1. What do you think?
   - Masturbation is second-rate sex.
   - Masturbation is okay if it is only a temporary program of self-control in order to avoid lust.
   - It is good practice for better sexual fulfillment in marriage.
   - It is a gift from God where we get a glimpse of future intimacy in marriage.
   - Though masturbation may cause no bodily harm, it could skew one's thinking.
   - If masturbation can take place without fantasy or lust, it is not sinful (some studies show that fantasizing does not always accompany masturbation).
   - Masturbation is a means of exploring one's body and how marvelously God has created it.
2. Why do you think masturbation is the most secretive sexual behavior?
3. For what reasons (besides feeling good) might people masturbate?

Some of God's Word

1. Study Genesis 38:8ff. Why do these verses not speak against masturbation?
2. Read Matthew 5:28. If masturbation involves fantasy, what does God's word say about it?
3. Early Jewish law forbade masturbation because it did not lead to procreation; however, for what other reason did God create us sexual (Song of Songs 3:1; Proverbs 5:18–19)?
4. Read Genesis 2:24. In what way is autoeroticism an incomplete form of "becoming one"?
5. Though there may be no clear passages from scripture condemning masturbation, what wisdom comes from St. Paul in 1 Corinthians 6:12?

Additional Video Clips for This Lesson (in Classroom or Home):

☑ *Sanctification* (Faith Visuals)

☑ *Purity Matters* (SermonSpice)

Completed: _____   _____

       Student Signature & Date of Completion   Parent/Teacher Signature & Date of Completion

Role Play: Pretend you're each of these characters in the cartoon. What is each saying?

Chapter 9

Sex and the Law

Truth: **In every state there are laws against certain sexual practices.**

Consider the following statements and questions that further speak to this truth:

1. Do you agree or disagree with the statement?
2. Does the statement prompt any special feelings within you (i.e., fear, laughter, unbelief)?
3. What additional questions come to mind after reading the statement?

Did You Know?

- Laws change over the years.
- In the nineteenth century, Nathaniel Hawthorne's novel *The Scarlet Letter* spoke of banishment and the wearing of a red letter "A" on a woman's dress for her sin of adultery. Why do you think very few states in the United States now have any laws against adultery?
- Up until a few years ago, there were laws against sodomy (male copulation). Do you think these laws should have been axed?
- Most states still consider prostitution illegal. Why do you think so?
- NAMBLA is an organization that asserts that men should have a right to have sex with boys. Why is such thinking so wrong?
- There are definite laws in most states against some sexual practices:
  - Having sex with someone under age—age of consent (i.e., in California, age eighteen)
  - Forcing someone into a sexual act during a date or a social engagement
  - Forcing a spouse to have sex without his/her consent
  - Having sex with someone who is closely related (incest)
  - Exhibitionism (exposing yourself) or voyeurism (peeking at others who are nude or having sex)
  - Buying, selling, or possessing child pornography
- Warning, young men! In more and more states, if during sex, at any time, your partner tells you to stop and you do not, charges can be brought against you for rape. If convicted, it means imprisonment and a label as detrimental as that spoken of in *The Scarlet Letter*.
- Once one is convicted of most sexual felonies, one is required to register as a sex offender. What first comes to your mind when you hear someone is a sex offender?
- Megan's Law was named after Megan Kanka in a New Jersey suburb, who was raped and murdered by a sex offender who lived across the street. (No one knew because at that time it was illegal to release sex offender information to the public.) Now many states require registrations of sex offenders and also that the names and whereabouts be published and made available. Such information often restricts a person's housing and employment opportunities.

Some Discussion

1. The young man was nineteen years of age. The young woman was seventeen years old. At a party one night, when both were intoxicated, oral copulation took place. Several weeks later, he was charged with having sex with someone underage. What do you think? Did the courts uphold the felony charge, even though it was only oral copulation? Yes, they did. Not only was he sentenced to one year in jail, but he was forced to register as a sex offender (for the rest of his life).

2. A survey posted in CosmoGirl.com reported that one in five teen girls and 18 percent of teen boys have sent or posted nude or seminude pictures or videos of themselves. Legal or illegal? What if an adult was caught in possession of these nude photos?

3. Discuss together some safeguards for every child and teenager online, specifically in relationship to MySpace, FaceBook, etc. For example, they should *never* give out identifying information such as name, address, school name, or telephone number to people they don't know.

Some Bible Truths

1. Despite what the "law of the land" might be (i.e., legalization of abortion), what law is greater than any civil law (Acts 5:29)? Think of laws that have passed, and though they are legal in the courts of the state, they are illegal in God's eyes (i.e., homosexual marriage).

2. There are other laws that are not contrary to God's word. In those cases, what must we do (Romans 13:1–7)?

3. Describe how rape (date, acquaintance, spousal) is contrary to everything spoken of in 1 Corinthians 13:4–8.

Additional Video Clips for This Lesson (in Classroom or Home):

☑ *Teen Dating Violence Prevention*, PSA (YouTube)

☑ *Causing Pain: Real Stories of Dating Abuse and Violence* (YouTube)

☑ *Hidden Secrets—Wrong* (Wing Clips)

☑ *Office Schmooze* (Faith Visuals)

Completed: _____   _____
            Student Signature & Date of Completion   Parent/Teacher Signature & Date of Completion

Role Play: Pretend you're the man in the cartoon. What do you think he's saying as he is running down the hill?

Chapter 10

The New Crack Cocaine: Pornography

Truth: **A leading addiction today is pornography, in large part because of the Internet.**

Consider the following statements and questions that further speak to this truth:

1. Do you agree or disagree with the statement?
2. Does the statement prompt any special feelings within you (i.e., fear, laughter, unbelief)?
3. What additional questions come to mind after reading the statement?

Did You Know?

- The front page (May 2009) of Reader's Digest read: *Parent Alert: Is Your Child Sexting?* Eleven- and twelve-year-old kids are taking compromising photos of themselves and sending them over their phones and computers. Do you know any young people your age who have sent inappropriate pictures of themselves on the phones or computer?

- Surveys show that 40 to 50 percent of all Internet users have visited an adult content site in the last year. Why?

- "Sex" is the most popular search term on the Internet. Why should this not surprise us? What other words do you think people have used to search for pornography?

- Jesus said to His disciples, "Things that cause people to sin are bound to come, but woe to that person through whom they come" (Luke 17:1). What does this passage say about those who provide pornography to people, such as those involved in the production of it?

- I have often called sexual addiction the "athlete's foot of the mind" because it never goes away. It is always asking to be scratched, promising relief, but to scratch it is to cause pain and to intensify the itch." What do you do when you get athlete's foot?
  Do you know of any medicine that might help with athlete's foot of the mind—pornography?

Some Discussion

1. Discuss the statement: "Sexual activity on the internet has fundamentally altered our sexuality ... barriers to sexual exploration were obliterated overnight."

2. Some experts are contending that "among young people, porn has become increasingly accepted, even socially acceptable." What avenues are now available via high technology that make it possible for anyone to "be socially acceptable"?

3. In a world where all values are equal, where everything is simply a matter of choice, why would narcissism (self-love) rule the day?

4. Studies tell us that 30 percent of all teenagers have visited Internet sites they don't want their parents to know about. The same studies show that 40 percent of all households have Internet filters. What are the advantages and disadvantages of such filters?

5. What are the consequences of a society where there are no limits to the availability of pornography?

Some Bible Truths

1. Read James 1:14–15. In what way do these verses describe the cycle of someone addicted to sexual pornography?

2. Whether it be alcoholism or pornography, any addiction is hard to get rid of by yourself. Most addicted people concur that they need help outside of what they can muster from within themselves. What help do Christians have that enables them to fight any battle against any addiction, including pornography (Ephesians 1:18–20)? Through holy baptism, we are resurrected to new possibilities. In what other ways do we continue to receive this "resurrection power"?

3. Summarize in your own words the meaning of 1 Thessalonians 4:3–5. Remember "sanctification" (being holy and right) comes as a result of "justification" (salvation through Jesus Christ).

Additional Video Clips for This Lesson (in Classroom or Home):

☑ *Dangers of Teen "Sexting,"* The Early Show, CBSNews.com

☑ *A Drug Called Pornography* (YouTube)

☑ *To Catch a Predator III*—Riverside, California, Dateline NBC.

☑ *The Pornography Rub* (SermonSpice)

Completed: _____   _____

　　　　　　Student Signature & Date of Completion　　　　　　Parent/Teacher Signature & Date of Completion

Role Play: What do you think? Are homosexuality or heterosexuality something like a DNA Diner, something you can pick and choose from?

Chapter 11

Not So Gay

Truth: **Homosexuality is a sexual orientation that cannot be proven to be genetic, gay, or in accordance with God's will.**

Consider the following statements and questions that further speak to this truth:

1. Do you agree or disagree with the statement?
2. Does the statement prompt any special feelings within you (i.e., fear, laughter, unbelief)?
3. What additional questions come to mind after reading the statement?

Did You Know?

- Gay? How do you think the term *gay* came to be used for those who are homosexual?

- Sex researcher Alfred Kinsey was wrong because of skewed research. He stated that 10 percent of the population are homosexual. More reliable research indicates that 3 to 5 percent of the population are gay. Do you think the percentage of those considering themselves "gay" has been increasing over the last few years? If so, why?

- In 1968, the APA (American Psychiatric Association) removed homosexuality as a mental disorder from their Diagnostic and Statistical Manual of Mental Disorders (DSM). By eliminating it as a disorder, what is the APA saying?

- There are two arenas of thinking regarding the origin of homosexuality—that it is either biologically or environmentally determined. What do you think? Is it biologically or environmentally determined?

- The thinking among some is that if it is genetically (biologically) determined, the person has no choice, so his or her behavior is not only condoned and blessed by God but should also be accepted by society. Every right should be afforded the homosexual, including the right to marry.

- There are no replicated scientific studies supporting specific biological causation for homosexuality (i.e., LeVay; Bailey and Pillard; Hamer; McFadden and Pasanen; Breedlove; Rahman, Kumari and Wilson). Why do you think the media over the years has announced that research has proven homosexuality to be biologically determined?

- Joseph Nicolosi, one of the leading researchers and therapists in homosexuality, believes that the homosexual condition is a developmental problem—and one that often results from early problems between father and son.

- Twenty-eight percent of homosexual males have one thousand or more partners in a lifetime. If so, what are the odds of getting STI infected?

- A major study found that not a single male couple (those who had entered a relationship with the pledge of sexual fidelity) was able to maintain sexual fidelity for more than five years.

Some Discussion

1. Even if one agreed that a person was genetically predisposed to homosexuality, would homosexual behavior be any more right than alcoholism? We do know for sure that one can be genetically predisposed to alcoholism.

2. Some would argue that if a person is born homosexual/lesbian, it would be wrong to try to get him/her to change. Agree or disagree?

3. Considering the fact that most homosexual relationships are so unstable, why would it be difficult to describe homosexuality as gay?

4. The definition of homophobia is the fear and hatred of homosexuals. In what way is that definition far different than how many people define it?

Some Bible Truths

1. Read Romans 1:18–27. St. Paul reminds us that when men mess up their relationship with God, they also disconnect with one another. What are the results of such disconnection according to these words?

2. How do Genesis 19:5 and Jude 7 speak to homosexuality?

3. How is the homosexual lifestyle spoken of in 1 Corinthians 6:9–11?

4. There are few myths more dangerous today than the one that says homosexuals are born the way they are, and even if they want to change, they can't. How does Ephesians 1:18–20 dispel such thinking?

5. Whether homosexual, bisexual, or heterosexual, it is important for a person to love everyone (even if you don't agree with his/her lifestyle). What does 1 John 4:19–21 say? However, is loving a person the same as tolerating wrongdoing?

Additional Resources for This Lesson (in Classroom or Home):

☑ *Understanding the Reasons for Being Gay—Lesbian* (David Kyle Foster, Internet)

☑ *On Wings Like Eagles* (Lifeline)

Completed: _____   _____

Student Signature & Date of Completion   Parent/Teacher Signature & Date of Completion

Role Play: What do you think might be the difference between the love of the two older people on the bench with the love of those standing up?

Chapter 12

What is Real Love?

Truth: **Real love is from God and best described in 1 Corinthians 13:4–8.**

Consider the following statements and questions that further speak to this truth:

1. Do you agree or disagree with the statement?
2. Does the statement prompt any special feelings within you (i.e., fear, laughter, unbelief)?
3. What additional questions come to mind after reading the statement?

Did You Know?

- The average sexually active person has had more than twenty-eight different sexual relationships by age thirty. What do you think? How many of those twenty-eight times do you think real love was involved?

- A dad told his son, "Son, an erection does not mean you're in love." *Sound crass?* Or is it the truth?

- "Why do you love him enough to marry him?" the pastor asks. She replies, "Because he makes me feel so good when we're together!" *So when the feelings come and go, is she no longer in love?*

- The average "tingly feelings"—feelings of strong sexual attraction (a romantic obsession)—lasts an average of two years according to expert Dr. Dorothy Tennov. Is it any wonder almost half of all marriages end in divorce? Could it be that the "tingly feelings" disappeared?

- Has the world gotten it all wrong? Usually we hear a lover express strong feelings about his/her lover, and love itself follows behind. Some would suggest love is not a feeling but a decision.

- What's wrong with this description of love? A boyfriend e-mailed his girlfriend:

  I love you so much. I would cross the desert for you, climb the highest mountain range, and swim the deepest ocean to be with you.

  I love you, sweetheart.

  Jacob

  PS, I'll be over tonight if the Laker's basketball game isn't very exciting.

- The title of the article read: "Friends, Friends with Benefits and the Benefits of the Local Mall." Often "friends with benefits" mean friends who favor each other with sex. Do you think love could be defined as something with benefits?

- For over 85 percent of people who marry today, part of their dating has included cohabitation—living together before the ceremony. The reason? "We want to see if it works before we tie the knot." But isn't real love unconditional?

- Grace, undeserved love and mercy, is absolutely necessary for love. Why? There is no perfect person.

Some Discussion

- ☑ One of the myths about love is that real love is never having to say you're sorry. What's wrong with such thinking? Can you think of some other myths about love?

- ☑ People often use the word *love* with regard to various levels and kinds of relationships. Is there anything different between saying, "I love my dog" and "I love my mother"?

- ☑ Love is a decision. Do you agree or disagree?

- ☑ What do you think the difference is between infatuation and love?

- ☑ Define the difference between "sex" and "making love."

Some Bible Truths

1. The word of God would suggest that love is a decision. To a church who had fallen out of love, Jesus recommends, "Remember (what your first love was like) … repent, and do the things you did at first" (Revelation 2:5). Isn't repentance required in every relationship, unless, of course, you know the "perfect person"? Is perfection ever possible here on earth, and if so, why did Jesus die on the cross for humankind's sins?
2. Read 1 Corinthians 13:4–8. Use these verses to define love. Make two columns: 1) What love is. 2) What love is not.
3. The writer of Ecclesiastes 4:10–12 describes the benefits of finding a good husband/wife. What are the benefits? Who is the third cord in the strand? Why is His presence essential for any good relationship?

Additional Video Clips for This Lesson (in Classroom or Home):

☑ *A Short Comedy about Real Love* (SermonSpice)

☑ *A Quick Explanation of What Real Love Is* (SermonSpice)

☑ *How Would You Define Real Love?* (SermonSpice)

☑ *License to Wed—Why Do You Love Her?* (Wing Clips)

Completed: _____   _____

Student Signature & Date of Completion   Parent/Teacher Signature & Date of Completion

In Summary

Our Creator, God the Father, wills the best for His created. Our Redeemer, Jesus Christ, through His life, death, and resurrection, assures us of the best—forgiveness and new life. Our Sanctifier, the Holy Spirit, makes this new life possible—eternity and "life more abundant" here on earth (John 10:10). "Abundant life" comes as we carry out God's will, including abstinence. Abstinence before marriage is His will for His people because He knows and seeks the best for His people—physically, emotionally, and spiritually.

Physically

1. It is the only sure way for the prevention of unwanted pregnancy and STDs or STIs. (The single biggest determinant for poverty in America is single parenthood.)
2. Following God's will in the use of the gift of sex is a sure way of preserving your "body [as] a temple of the Holy Spirit" (1 Corinthians 6:19).

Emotionally

1. Different from animals, humans are relational. Healthy relationships consist of commitment and grace. Without these elements, sex becomes nothing more than what it is for animals—a means to an end. Sex without love eventually leaves one feeling used, empty, and lonely.
2. "Yada sex"—God's design—promises feelings of being fully known and knowing another person. Relationally, it builds trust and security.

Spiritually

1. Living outside of God's will never promises blessings. "One who sows to please his sinful nature … reap(s) destruction" (Galatians 6:8).
2. Living within God's will—becoming one flesh as husband and wife—promises blessings: "God saw all that He had made, and it was very good" (Genesis 1:31).

Promises have always been an important part of maintaining a civilized society—one that is moral and just. In everything from the promises made at a wedding to those spoken in the courtroom, promises hold people accountable. They help guide them into the decisions they make and serve as mental reminders to carry them out. Promises that are kept help build trust and a sense of security in marriages, families, and society.

A promise of abstinence is as important as any promise made. It denotes a decision to remain sexually abstinent until marriage. This includes intercourse as well as outercourse. Such a promise is possible for the Christian because Jesus makes it possible. St. Paul's promise to us is: "If God is for us, who can be against us? He who did not spare His own Son, but gave Him up for us all—how will He not also, along with Him, graciously give us all things?" (Romans 8:31–32). He will help us keep our promises—including a promise of abstinence. We can be assured, God keeps His promises—every one of them. "For no matter how many promises God has made, they are 'yes' in Christ" (2 Corinthians 1:20). The resurrection of Jesus is a guarantee that every promise He makes is sure! Through holy baptism, we are resurrected to new possibilities, including keeping promises of abstinence.

As a parent(s) and a tween or teenager, after you have studied the twelve lessons, you might want to do some of the following things:

■ Plan a special time when a promise of abstinence is made.
■ Purchase a special ring (or other piece of jewelry) to present to your tween or teenager as a reminder of his/her promise.
■ Go out for a special dinner to celebrate the event.
■ Special people, such as, godparents, might also be invited.

If the program is used in the church, these promises might be made in a worship service. The young people and their parents make promises and the congregation also celebrates and affirms them with its own promise. A congregational celebration elevates the promise these young people make to a level that is as important as other promises made in the church (i.e., a wedding, ordination).

Do Abstinence Programs Work?

The question many are asking is whether abstinence teaching makes any difference. The National Longitudinal Study of Adolescent Health has shown that young people who make abstinence pledges substantially delay the initiation of sexual activity, have fewer sexual partners, are more likely to marry, and have lower rates of out-of-wedlock births. The research also shows that the most effective abstinence teaching takes place when there are two givens: 1) a continuous sex education from cradle to grave (not just a one-time shot); 2) education that is values-based. The February 2010 *Archives of Pediatric & Adolescent Medicine* reported that an extensive federal study found that students who take classes emphasizing abstinence are less likely to have sex than those who take classes teaching safe sex.

Some must resources to help every parent and teacher further discuss sex/sexuality with young people are the following:

- Roger Sonnenberg, Human *Sexuality: A Christian Perspective.* St. Louis, MO: Concordia Publishing House (CPH), 1998.
- Concordia Sex Education Series, *Learning about Sex for the Christian Family*, six different books for different ages (*Why Boys and Girls Are Different*; *Where Do Babies Come From?*; *How You Are Changing*; *Sex and the New You*; *Love, Sex, and God*; *How to Talk Confidently with Your Child about Sex*), updated and divided for boys/ girls, CPH, St. Louis, MO, 2008.
- Pam Stenzel, *Sex, Love & Relationships* (a four-part DVD series), Core Alliance, 1998.
- Pam Stenzel, *Love Lessons—Purity Is Possible Curriculum*-Faith Based, Core Alliance, 2009.
- Doug Herman, *Sex Appeal, Pure Revolution*, Littleton, CO, 1998.

Over the last thirteen years, *Our Savior Lutheran Church*, Arcadia, California, has held what is called the Lovefest. It is a weekend for parents and students to learn more about sex and their sexuality. There is always a featured speaker (e.g., Pam Stenzel), a large variety of workshops for parents and students, and a special worship service on Sunday morning. This event has grown over the years to the point where it has outgrown the available facilities. For more information about this event, contact the author.

A Pledge Suggestion for the Young Person

I,_____, in the presence of God and you, promise to remain sexually abstinent until marriage. This includes all forms of sexual activity, from intercourse to outercourse. I choose to make this pledge because I believe it is God's will for me. I also know I will be unable to keep this promise on my own; however, I will draw on the power of the Holy Spirit for needed help. I celebrate this day and give God thanks for having been led to make this decision. I give God all glory and praise.

A Response from the Parent(s)

We celebrate with you on this day and pledge you our support in helping you keep this promise. We will encourage you with our words and actions. We will pray for you, knowing that the promise you made will not be easy to keep in the world in which we live. The devil, the world, and your flesh will tempt you; however, know that you have a stronger power. United to Him through holy baptism, you are resurrected to new possibilities—including keeping the promise you just made. We are so thankful to God for this day and celebrate with you.

(If a ring or other piece of jewelry is used.)
(As the ring is placed on the finger) This is a ring. We purchased it especially for you to wear. Just as a wedding ring is a symbol of promises made, so let this ring be a symbol of the promises you have made today and your promised faithfulness.

A Response from the Congregation

We, the members of____, join you and your parents in celebration. Our prayer for you is "that the eyes of your heart may be enlightened in order that you know … His incomparably great power (available to you) … that power is like the working of His mighty strength, which he exerted in Christ when He raised Him from the dead and seated Him at His right hand in the heavenly realms" (Ephesians 1:18–20). We join in thanksgiving to God for this day, for His promise of love and forgiveness, and for the promise to help us keep the promises we make, including the ones we have heard today.

Certificate of Completion and Promise

I _____ on this day____have completed the abstinence course and promise in the presence of God to remain sexually abstinent until marriage. This includes all forms of sexual activity, from intercourse to outercourse. I choose to make this pledge because I believe it is God's will for me. I also know I will be unable to keep this promise on my own; however, I will draw on the power of the Holy Spirit for needed help. I celebrate this day and give God thanks for having been led to make this decision. I give God all glory and praise.

We (parents and others in attendance) celebrate with you and pledge our support in helping you keep this promise. We promise to encourage you with our words and actions. We promise to pray for you, knowing that the promise you made will not be easy to keep in the world in which we live. The devil, the world, and your flesh will tempt you; however, know that you have a power stronger. United to Him through holy baptism, you are resurrected to new possibilities—including keeping the promise you just made. We are so thankful to God for this day and celebrate with you. (signatures below)

Printed in the United States
By Bookmasters